Ugler Lee

Ugler Lee

Poems by

Charles Rammelkamp

Cover design by Shay Culligan
Cover art by Abby Rammelkamp

ISBN: 978-1-952326-44-8

Kelsay Books
502 South 1040 East, A-119
American Fork, Utah, 84003

"As Bokonon tells us, 'It is never a mistake to say good-bye.'"
—Kurt Vonnegut, *Cat's-Cradle*

This book is in memory of

Julian Rammelkamp, 1917-1994
David Rammelkamp, 1948-2005
Mabel Rammelkamp, 1919-2012
Robert Rammelkamp, 1952-2016

Acknowledgments

Pacific Coast Journal: "Sarcasm"

The Mid-American Poetry Review: "After My Brother's Funeral,"
"Illinois Ice Storm"

Songs of the San Joaquin: "The Empty Nest," "The Ambassadors"

Main Channel Voices: "The Bequest" "Immortal"

Iodine Poetry Review: "Mishebarach," "Shallow Roots"

Exit 13: "New Year's Eve 2005"

Waterways: "Christmas Cheer," "O Muse," "Legacy," "He Adored
Her," "The Minyan," "Give Us This Day," "Meeting My
Mother in the Hereafter"

Green Hills Literary Lantern: "The Bed"

Colere: "Beets"

Barbaric Yawp: "A Shanda," "Suicide Poem"

Slipstream: "Mixed Signals," "On Their Way to Elsewhere"

Pilgrimage: "The Arrival of Spring"

Red River Review: "Politics"

Foliate Oak: "The Bond," "After My Mother Died"

Pudding House: "Lullabies"

The 5-2 Crime Blog: "Good Cop / Bad Cop," "Home Again"

Main Street Rag: "Threshold"

Star 82 Review: "The Gematria of Five Sisters"

Body Verses: "Ugler Lee"

Homestead Review: "Peaches and Cream," "Gemini"

Glimpse: "Averting a Calamity"

Leaping Clear: "Zen Riddle"

Contents

Part Three: Dreaming of Warning Signs

Part Four: Palliative Care

Part One: Right After Breakfast

The Arrival of Spring

"It was the time of year when men
start to wear short-sleeve shirts,"
is how my grandmother began
the story of falling in love
with my grandfather,
both in their thirties by then,
a decorous tale of a midday meeting
in a bank on Main Street
between a schoolteacher and a salesman
in a small town in Tennessee.

But it was as if they were code words
for an elaborate mating ritual,
the tail-lifting of the female,
the strutting and preening of the male,
the choreography of desire and seduction.

She spoke with the fond indifference
of recollection, like the narrator
of a nature show on public TV,
but in her voice I imagined I could hear
the cries of cats in heat
in distant midnight backyards,
smell the spray of musk animals emit
to tease the sexual sense.

"At first he didn't know who I was,"
she recalled. "I could tell by the way
his eyes popped out like a bullfrog's
when he tried to greet me by name,
but he never let on
he'd forgotten our schooldays together,
couldn't exactly put a name on me,
say who I was."

He came calling the next day,
and in the autumn they were married.
Within a year they had their only child,
a daughter. My mother.

Homeless and Hungry

During the Great Depression my grandmother
used to make sandwiches for hobos
who came to her backyard gate
down in beat East Saint Louis.

They asked for work for day wages,
and sometimes she'd find an odd job
they could perform: something broken
they could fix or some yard work,
cutting grass, trimming hedges, raking leaves,
but mainly she gave them something to eat.

Soon enough, word got around
a lady in the neighborhood
made sandwiches for tramps,
and they started drifting to the gate
like fallen leaves driven by the wind,
until she finally had to draw the line.

"Sorry, I don't need any work done today,"
she'd say, and they'd say,
"Well, do you think you could give a fella some food?"

Her husband was a lucky one,
a job in a meat-packing plant.
He worked all night, slept during the day.

Sometimes the beggars became belligerent,
driven to desperation and threats,
but she wasn't afraid of them.
She just said she was sorry and closed the gate.

She felt bad for all those homeless men.
It certainly wasn't their fault.
But people will always take advantage of you
if you let them.

The First Time I Tasted

The first time I tasted pecan pie
was the week after my grandmother died.
She lay upstairs in her bed dying for weeks,
calling to Jesus to take her to him.

She'd always implored and cajoled Jesus,
prayed to him, sang him songs, asked favors,
fingered sinners, blessed the meal. Now
her plea took on the tones of delirium, orgasm.

She moaned in her pain, eager for death,
urging her soul to depart from her flesh,
to sail up to Heaven to be with Him,
to look down at the rest of us below.

On Christmas Day an expectant silence
filled the hallway outside her room.
We tiptoed past, afraid to disturb
the drama unfolding behind the door.

My grandmother's struggle with annihilation,
her urge for extinction balanced against
a Sunday school belief in immortality,
eternity spent on a fleecy cloud of salvation.

Then my father heard the death rattle
like rolled metal marbles clicking and ticking.
We all let out our breath, only then aware
how tense we had all been.

In the week between Christmas and New Year's
people brought food and sent sympathy cards.
Among the pies on the dining room table
one was studded with a brown, nutty crust.

The rich gluey filling gummed my mouth.
A new sensation, a new taste. Gone forever
the butter-soaked slices of cornbread
and the coconut cakes my grandmother made.

Gone, too, the strident admonitions to obey
the harsh rules made up by somebody named God,
strict rules which only she seemed to know.
Gone forever my silent resistance to her exhortations.

Christmas Cheer

Doctor Taylor stumbled
into the living room littered
with toys, board games,
bright tattered wrapping paper,
a blast of cold winter air
circling him like his whiskey fumes.

He'd been summoned
from his own celebrations,
enjoying the holiday
with his family across town,
daughter Karen back home
from her first year at the university.

"She's upstairs." My father's funereal voice
blew away any lingering awkwardness.
Doctor Taylor followed him
to my grandmother's room,
holding onto the handrail for support,
trundling like a beaver
in his heavy winter overcoat,
leaving a suspenseful silence behind.

Several minutes later they returned,
Doctor Taylor, weaving slightly,
formally shook my father's hand,
patted my mother's heaving shoulder.
He let himself out the door,
back into the cold Christmas night.
He hadn't even removed his coat,
having come to certify
my mother was now an orphan.

The Past

"He made me strip naked for his friends,"
his mother confided to her younger friend,
recollecting her older brother,
dead fifty years to the day,
the hurt and anger
throbbing in her voice,
raw as an open wound.

A day in August marks a death,
but so much lives within it, the shame
a ninety-three-year-old woman still feels
for something that happened
over three-quarters of a century before,
evident in the angry sheen of her ancient eyes.

"His friends!" she spat, some unarticulated memory
causing her eyes to flash again, thunderbolts
ripping into a time that hadn't gone away.
"How he loved those cruds."

More than just the nude episode, Joanne realized
history bubbling up like sulfuric acid in a beaker.
This could have happened yesterday.
It could have happened right after breakfast.

The Bond

After all these years the pain
seared as fresh and vivid as a brand,
flaring up in my mother's eyes, bright
as sparks flying from an anvil.

"Life with Mother was hell," she told Joanne,
recalling those bleak post-war years
she and her husband and their toddler
had lived with her parents
while her husband substituted at the high school,
tried desperately to find a job in his field,
her mother critical of everything
she did, aspired to, believed.

"Even after the tenure-track job came along
and we left town as if fleeing a dictator,
I felt her tugging at my sleeve,
gnarled fingers clutching at my elbow,
yanking me away from my life.

"And then, of course, she followed us
after my dad's heart attack,
widowhood giving her carte blanche
to meddle in my life.
Even though she had her own apartment,
she never felt she had to knock:
what was mine was hers;
she'd given birth to me, after all.

"And finally, after the fall, the broken hip,
she moved in with us,
took over the guest bedroom,
demanded I wait on her,
cater to her every whim,
the Queen, the *grande dame*—
'just like I took care of you,'"
Mom's voice imitating a Disney witch.

Now in her nineties, her mother
dead nearly half a century,
still, it sounded as if
this could have happened last week,
my mother waiting for an apology
she knew would never come.

Part Two: Ugler Lee

Alma Mater

My parents met at Illinois College
in the waning years of the Great Depression,
over a decade before I was born:
the mother of their souls the same.

On a scholarship from East Saint Louis,
my mother arrived at Illinois College
the year my father became a junior,
born and bred in that same small town,
Jacksonville, on the very campus:
my grandfather having been president
of the Hilltop college the year of my father's birth, 1917,
dying in office fifteen years later.

Built on a ritual mound of the Kickapoo tribe,
the oldest college in the state
also gave birth to the soul
of the great anti-intellectual populist,
three-time Democratic presidential candidate
(three-time loser)
and laughingstock of the Scopes Monkey trial,
William Jennings Bryan,
with whom my father's father
had had a famous falling-out
over "tainted money" from Andrew Carnegie,
Bryan resigning from the board of trustees,
threatening to expunge his name
from the rolls of the graduates,
to which my grandfather replied
he could resign if he chose, but
it was a matter of history he could not retract:
Illinois College had given birth to his soul.

Born in Jacksonville, too,
I moved with my family to Michigan
even before my first memory—
my mother, my father, my older brother and my twin—
returning after high school
to the scene of my birth
so my soul could be born.

Found Poem: *East St. Louis Journal,* Sunday, March 1, 1942

Marriage Is Announced
Mabel Tippitt Becomes Bride
of Julian Rammelkamp in Florida

Mr. and Mrs. Addison Tippitt, Fairview,
announce the marriage of their daughter,
Miss Mabel Alvera,
to Corporal Julian Sturtevant Rammelkamp,
son of Mrs. Charles Henry Rammelkamp,
Jacksonville, Ill.
The marriage took place Wednesday
at the First Methodist Church in Tampa.

Both young people,
whose engagement was announced three years ago,
are graduates of Illinois College,
where Corporal Rammelkamp's father was president
from 1905 to 1932.
The bride majored in French and psychology.
Corporal Rammelkamp majored in history.

The couple's plans are indefinite.
Corporal Rammelkamp has been in army service
since last August
after two years of graduate work at Brown University,
preparatory to his doctor's degree.
He is now stationed at a Southern post.
His bride is society editor of *The Journal.*
She will continue with her work
for the duration of the war.

Smalltown Pride

"Welcome to Jacksonville,
Home of Ken Norton,"
the billboard greeted you in 1970,
the man who defeated Ali
but was never champ.

This is how a small town
presents itself to the world,
thinking perhaps to lift itself
from the monotonous anonymity
of town after town strung out
along the state highways
like beads on a chain.

A film of glamour,
dust from a moth's wings,
settles on the town,
mirage-like as moonlight.

"Welcome to Homer,
birthplace of 1988 Olympic Silver Medalist—"
but you've driven past
before the actual name registers.

Illinois Ice Storm

"She was married the year before the storm,"
someone remembers,
gauging distance, proportion.
"It was colder than the winter
the ice took down all the trees,
snapped the barbed wire branches
of the Osage Orange like so many matchsticks."

In the midst of all that loss
the need for meaning, to locate ourselves,
know a sense of purpose,
keen and cold as ice.

Good Cop/Bad Cop

"Your mother doesn't want another cat,"
I tell my children, shrugging helplessly
when they ask if we can't get another.
A look of pleading fills their eyes,
but they already know the answer.
It's been two years since Grover died,
our sweet ancient tabby.
Nothing I can do about it, my mute defense.

I recall the last five years of Grover's life,
curled in a corner, struggling to his feet,
the pills I forced down his throat every morning,
turds we stepped on in the dark,
puddles of urine and vomit on the floor.

My father was distant when I was a kid,
deep in the concerns of his research
like an explorer in a cave with a flashlight –
permissive, lenient to his children,
leaving discipline to his wife.

Slogging through the muck of parenting,
sleeves rolled up, Mom laid down the law,
set the curfews, spelled out the consequences.

A Poem Inspired by My Mother's Walker

It's nothing shameful Rosemary thinks,
stepping into the weightless aluminum scaffolding,
like the shiny silver exoskeleton
of some extinct four-legged creature.
At least I have the confidence
to walk across the room now.

She still remembers the sound,
the feel of her hip crunching
when she landed on the cement floor,
waiting in endless agony
for Carl, the building janitor,
in the basement laundry room.

At least I'm not wheelchair-bound.
Rose thinks of Mildred Tidd,
her neighbor three doors down,
Or have to lug that oxygen tank
like a scuba diver,
the way Helen O'Toole does,
thankful she'd given up cigarettes
when she was pregnant with Robert,
hearing again the awful sound of Helen's wheezes,
lungs raked by emphysema.

Or worse, she shudders, gripping
the rough rubber handlebars,
slowly making her way to the apartment door,
I could be like Herb Moskowitz,
who can't even control his bladder any more.
His daughter has to hold his youknowwhat
when he goes to the bathroom.
He says he wants to kill himself.

But the look on her son's face
when she greets Robert at the door
makes her think of the forlorn rhythmic clanking
when she gets up to use the toilet
in the stillness of the night.

"Mom, you look wonderful!"
Robert gushes past her shoulder.

Riddle of the Sphinx

"Listen," the old lady said to her son,
voice matter-of-fact as a bedpan.
"When I get out of this nursing home,
I'm making damn sure I don't come back."

The desperate determination behind her eyes
fixed Charles in place
like a sheet-covered corpse strapped to a gurney.

"I won't compromise you
in some illegal complicity;
I won't even let you know,"
she went on, watching his face,
"But I'm going to lay in a supply
of whatever it takes to kill me
next time I fall and can't get back up."

What could Charles say?
Don't say that!
Don't talk that way!
It's really not that bad, Ma!
But he knew it *was* that bad.

Certain as Oedipus
solving the riddle and saving Thebes,
he stared at his frail mother.
Four legs, two legs, three—
then none at all.

The Fugitive

Five years after we buried my brother
my mother continues her fight—
unable to dress, cook, bathe,
use the toilet
without help,
she's assembled a team,
neighbors, friends,
friends of friends,
to assist her with the basics—
for a fee, of course.

Sixteen years after we buried my father
she schemes her way
to a sort of self-reliance—
avoiding the disinfectant atmosphere
of the nursing home,
uniformed nurses, drooling roommates—
resourceful as a prison escapee
dodging the feds.

How much longer
will she be able
to cover her tracks?

Missing Persons

"Who took the picture?"
my mother murmurs like the surf,
the four of us standing by the lake,
squinting into the sun.

Usually, someone's missing,
behind the camera;
usually me.

But there we all stand,
my wife, my two daughters and me,
the lake behind us,
a whitecap rearing up behind us,
as if the upper lip of the lake had lifted,
when the photographer told us to smile.

My mother examines the snapshot,
as if she might find a signature,
a thumbprint, a tell-tale sign.

"I don't know," I confess.
"I can't remember."
It feels like negligence,
something I should have noted.

At ninety, my mother's lost
so many of her contemporaries,
she's like the lone survivor from a shipwreck
stumbling on the beach.

Give Us This Day

Give us this day our daily date,
I think, wondering what
today's Hebrew equivalent might be.
Happens every August.
My father died on the 24th,
but when does his Hebrew yahrzeit fall?
Not that he was a Jew, and not that I'm lighting candles,
but Elul 17 flits around the Gregorian field
like a grasshopper,
leaping from one spot to another year by year.

I became a Jew on Shevat 16 in 5743,
better known as January 30, 1983,
fifty years to the day
Hitler rose to power.

My daughters' birthdays,
both in the month of Kislev,
come only seventeen days apart,
Hebrew time,
a full three weeks the way
we normally count,
one in November, one in December.

Of course, in one calendar
the day ends at the eerie midnight hour,
the other more serenely at sunset.
Mine usually ends somewhere in between.

Sarcasm

"And they said unto Moses: 'Because there were no graves in Egypt, hast thou taken us away to die in the wilderness? wherefore hast thou dealt thus with us, to bring us forth out of Egypt?'"

—*Exodus* 14:11

"You ungrateful little shit,"
my father snarled,
worse than a slap to the face,
when in response
to his question
about whether I envied
Brent Robinson for the car
his parents had given him,
I'd aimed for arch wit, sneering,
"No, I really like
waiting half an hour for you
to pick me up after school."

Instead of amusing him
with my droll humor,
as I'd intended,
I'd offended him,
pissed him off.
And then I couldn't just
explain the joke, could I?

New Year

"Are you retired?"
the hygienist enquired,
polite chitter-chatter
before scraping and polishing
my teeth.

"Just taking the week off
between Christmas and New Year's,"
I replied, wondering what
it was about me that said,
"out to pasture."
My bald head with the gray fringe
like the ragged fur of a dying mammal?
The jeans, the flannel shirt?
Somebody sensing the same thing
about me had given me red suspenders
as a Christmas gift.
At least I wasn't wearing those.

Behind her surgical mask,
Renee looked to be
on the old end of young,
somewhere in her thirties.

I remembered my father's chagrin
when I was Renee's age
and he told me one of his freshman
girls had gushed she loved him.
"You remind me of my grandfather."

40

The Practical Joke

Freiermuth, my father's former
college colleague called
from his asylum in Kalamazoo—
to harangue Pop about complicated political plots,
government thought-control conspiracies,
fabricated memories, hallucinated schemes;

for instance, his insistence, like a facial tic,
that the college president
staged elaborate private orgies
with innocent college girls,
ritualistic Aztec sacrifices, virgins
stolen from dorm rooms
by CIA agents posing as KGB spies.
He'd go on about the gold-covered altars on which
the virgins were deflowered and disemboweled.

My father feigned interest,
but pleading an impending appointment,
gave the guy the telephone number
of a humorless mutual acquaintance,
the most sanctimonious man I'd ever met:
a Methodist preacher, Howard Peterson,
who constantly condemned drunkenness and adultery
with something of a cuckold's
impotent rage and self-righteousness.
So full of pompous theoretical remedies
for the character flaws he saw in others.

Freiermuth thanked my father,
then hung up to call his new victim,
collect, just as this one
had been on my dad's dime.

A mixture of mischief and relief
gleamed wetly in Pop's brown eyes.
He could almost hear Howard's smug superiority,
drowned by the sound of his heart pounding,
as he realized he was trapped
in conversation with this madman.

You couldn't say my father
didn't have a wicked sense of humor.

Politics

The summer cottage was lit like a Dutch painting,
dim kerosene lamps capped
by opaque glass shades,
a crackling fire in a distant hearth,
light licking brief whips
against the bare pine walls.
My father and uncle huddled together,
shadowy figures talking politics
as if in some deep conspiracy—
Nixon, LBJ, Vietnam, law and order.
Insubstantial as memories,
shadows within shadows within shades.

It was like the Vermeer painting
of two women sitting in a kitchen
whom you spy through a doorway,
intrusive as a voyeur.
One holds a lute in her lap;
both wear bonnets.

You aren't supposed to be here!
A little voice, thrilling, whispered, warned.
This is not for you to hear!
Not the subject, not the politics,
but the give-and-take
between my father and his brother,
the smoldering violence of their disagreement,
about to burst into flames,
like a log collapsing in the fireplace
with a deafening *whoosh!*
shooting up a mouthful of flames,
lighting up the room
in brilliant uproar.

Ugler Lee

"Ugler lee," my father groaned,
frown lines breaking out around his mouth,
scratching his head, private commentary
when something unspeakable happened—
cataclysmic weather events, irreversible illness,
tragic, pointless death—
a kind of onomatopoeic observation
for something for which there are no words.

The night my grandmother died, Christmas Eve 1970,
we'd all sat down to a somber feast
on what was meant to be a festive occasion,
but nobody had much of an appetite,
waiting, waiting for a sign,
as if magi seeking a guiding star.
After dinner, my mother discovered
her mother was no longer breathing
upstairs in the room in which she lay.

"Ugler lee," my father muttered,
forehead going to wrinkles
as if a windowpane struck by a rock,
picking up the phone to dial the doctor.

Beets

"Pink, red or smoky brown urine may be caused by the consumption of
beets."

—*Medical Encyclopedia*

Among the produce provided
by the community agriculture outfit
to which we belong,
beets.

When my wife mentioned
the pink stain of her urine
the morning after
we'd eaten a beet recipe,

I remembered my mother
telling me my father
asked her if they'd had beets
for dinner the previous evening

a week before he was hospitalized—
shortness of breath—
two before he died—
massive heart failure—
three before the autopsy results
indicated pancreatic cancer.

They hadn't,
but that was all
he said to her about it.

Ashes to Ashes

In the funeral home
I waited that hot August morning
for my mother to return
from saying her final good-bye
to my father
before they cremated his remains.

She told me I didn't have to accompany her,
and I don't know
if I chose not to go
out of respect for her privacy,
as if I might intrude
on some final intimacy,
or if it was out of some fear
and ultimate repugnance,
telling myself I was giving
back some final dignity
by declining to view the lifeless flesh.

When she finally returned
from the bowels
of the funeral home,
like Odysseus returning from Hades,
she told me it wasn't really him there,
still so overcome with her sorrow.

After the memorial service,
we went to the cemetery,
but by that time
the little casket containing my father's ashes
had already been sealed underground
and all at once, I felt an irrational urge
to dive in there with him,
to say my own final good-bye.

The Wife's Good-bye

I wanted to see him one final time
before they put his body
into the oven and gave me back
an urn of ashes.

But when I saw him there,
I knew he was gone.
He'd already said his good-byes,
wasn't around any longer to hear mine.

Stretched out in the casket,
a blanket over him.
I touched his face,
but I didn't touch him.
I kissed his cheek,
but I didn't kiss him.

Grateful I'd offered our son
the option to stay behind,
I remembered the morning
he walked into our bedroom,
a boy of fourteen,
and saw my husband hunched on his knees
in a position of prayer,
his face between my legs.

He turned around and left the room,
pretending he hadn't seen a thing,
and my husband jumped to my side,
curling into a fetal ball, pretending
he was really asleep,
and I lay like a patient
spread out on an operating table,
pretending I, too, was asleep.

None of us ever mentioned
that summer morning incident.
Why would we?
What was there to say?
Soon I forgot all about it.
Until now.

On Their Way to Elsewhere

On our way to Lake Michigan
we stopped in my hometown
to visit my father's grave,
the headstone just erected
the previous August, minus the dates.

Riverside Cemetery slopes
to the banks of the Kalamazoo
gradual as a life winding down to old age,
then drops sharply,
a steep dive to the shore.

Below my father's headstone
flocks of Canadian Geese filled
the sloping lawn, feathered paperweights
resting up for the next part of the trip,
journeying back home for the summer.
It looked like an invasion
but they'd be gone in a few days.

Carved into the marble my mother's
name beside my father's,
the date of her birth
followed by a hyphen,
next to her husband's
dates of birth and death,
neat as a pair of parentheses.

Bed and Breakfast

My daughter asked permission
to sleep with my mother last night.
Though the decision was hers,
I let her sleep in my mother's bed.

I had this idea my mother
would really like a human companion
lying in sleep beside her,
the first time since her husband died.

I thought it might answer some need
she wasn't even fully conscious
of having had or would find
too dangerous to acknowledge
even in private,
for all the implications it brings.

It's been eight months
since my father died
so suddenly and unexpectedly,
her bed partner for more
than half a century.

Passing her room the next morning,
I saw them lying there,
my mother and my child,
curled together like a bear and cub.

I tiptoed down the stairs
to start the coffee,
feeling I might have glimpsed
something like redemption
in the corner of my eye.

Lethe

When Hersh told me five years ago
at my daughter's bat mitzvah
he'd known my father fifty years
before, when he was a student at Harvard,
my father his History TA,
it felt like a gift from the dead,
something rescued from oblivion.

He'd heard the rabbi announce
the flowers on the bimah honored
the memory of Julian Rammelkamp.
"Same one," I answered the elderly gentleman
who introduced himself at the kiddush.

But lately, Hersh has been calling me Richard,
not really close to my name, Charles,
other than the "char."
I'm too embarrassed to correct him.
But it feels as if something's slipping
ineluctably back into oblivion.

Legacy

"If it wasn't for your dad," Paul insisted,
"I don't know what would have become of me."
When the guy I'd met at the gym,
an editor for the local newspaper,
learned my name and who my father was—
a guy I'd casually discussed
sports and politics with for years,
either changing into gym togs
or back into street clothes—
my father, dead almost a decade,
came back to life for me,
the mensch and mentor
who'd helped more than one person
find his way.

"I was a hippie in college.
I mean, I was a good student,
liked to write,
loved your dad's classes,
but I had no idea
what I wanted to do with my life."

After a year on a commune in Oregon,
Paul had returned to the Midwest,
the town with the college where my father taught,
talked with his old prof.,
who made some calls,
got Paul into journalism school.

"And the rest is history," Paul marveled,
his voice ironic with the cliché
but no less sincere because of it.

Last of the Generation

When the email came
halfway across the country
with my uncle's name in the subject line,
I knew even before I opened it
the news it contained.

He'd passed away in his sleep
the night before.
His wife found him already cold
when she went to join him
an hour after he'd gone to bed.

"Just like your father,"
my mother noted on the phone,
when I told her Uncle Ted had died,
remembering how Pop keeled over
in the emergency room
where ten years before he'd driven himself,
complaining of shortness of breath.
 "They all died quickly,
without a lot of suffering."

"Just like Aunt Edith," I agreed,
who'd been standing on the scales
at the health club
when she crumpled over,
a massive heart attack,
a third of a century ago.

"Every one of them," she repeated,
as if writing the final line to an epitaph.
The family she'd married into
sixty-five years before,
all of them now gone.

Part Three: Dreaming of Warning Signs

The Empty Nest

The day after my wife and I
left our younger daughter at her dorm,
Abby heard a commentator on public radio
reflect on taking his child to college;
he missed the kid
because she'd always been
a buffer between him and his wife.

When my wife asked me
if this was how I felt,
I replied, "Not necessarily."

"Not necessarily?"
Abby's tone bordered on hysteria,
as if I'd said I didn't believe in God,
or the Bush years had been a success.
Clearly, the wrong answer.

But all I meant was
I could see
where the guy was coming from,
as if the hobby they'd shared
for over two decades –
stamp-collecting, film noir, bird-watching –
had been stripped away from them,
and all that was left
was washing dinner dishes,
paying the bills.

Immortal

"Your Aunt Edith died young,"
Uncle Harold pointed out,
testy, as a child interrupted in its nap.
"Heart attack.
And your grandfather.
He was only in his fifties, too.
Cerebral thrombosis."

Married to my father's older sister,
and already over seventy,
Uncle Harold lay in the chaise lounge
in the late afternoon shade
on the porch beside the lake,
warning me, smug college student,
my life was not endless.

Looking at the liver spots
discoloring his arthritic hands,
the wrinkles in his face,
his wavy white hair,
I forgave him.

The Bed

"My neck is killing me,"
my wife sighs in the three a.m. silence,
streetlight seeping
through the curtains.

We squirm under the covers,
adjust the pillows,
including the one
she keeps between her legs
for the sciatica.

My own left shoulder throbs
from slumping on my side in my sleep
in a middle-aged fetal curl.

As we drift back to sleep
I remember my father-in-law,
the last twenty years of his life
sleeping in a recliner
because of his back.

My mother likewise sleeps
in an adjustable chair—
she's unable to rise
once she lies down.

Ah, the bed,
once it spawned
a riot of fantasies,
women spread-eagled and moaning,
wet with desire.

Now I fall asleep,
mindful of the hazards of repose,
dreaming of warning signs,
a use-by date,
a skull and crossbones—
a series of cautions,
a list of consequences.

Mixed Signals

Back in the Sixties,
when everybody smoked cigarettes,
my pixyish blond Aunt Sally,
fresh from the shower,
a towel wrapped about her,
modest but provocative,
sprayed her hair (Alberto VO 5),
a butt dangling from her mouth.

The hairspray ignited,
her head a halo of fire.
She screamed, the smoke
rolling under the vanity,
her towel falling away.

Eight years old,
I stood outside the bathroom,
door half open,
watching my aunt grab the towel,
smother her head,
as if in some crazy purification rite,
killing the flames before
any serious damage.

Just a kid who assumed
all endings were happy,
I howled at the sight:
my naked aunt, towel over head
like a shroud, fear distorting her features.

Aunt Sally's open hand
caught me across the cheek,
knocking me backward.

Recovering her composure,
she pulled me to her,
pressing my face against her naked breasts,
the confusing scent of singed hair, tobacco,
her sex wafting up from her lap,
as I watched the small flame
from the linoleum under the vanity
where the cigarette had rolled.

A Shanda

"You're going to write a poem about it, aren't you,"
my wife barked, an accusation, not a question.
Her brother had just beaten up his wife,
dragged Leah by the hair
out of their Saint Louis apartment,
kicked her down a flight of stairs
like a thug in a gangster movie.
The neighbors called the cops.
Barry spent the night in jail.

"I hadn't really thought about it," I lied,
"but now that you mention it,
it does present a compelling scene,
though I'm not sure
what lesson could be derived from it."

"How about what a shit Barry is,"
Amy suggested, bitter as spoiled milk.
"How about this isn't the first time,
just the first time the asshole's been caught,
the first time he hit Leah
in front of their children?"

"I still don't see the point,"
I said, convincing myself
not to write the poem,
"beyond the obvious condemnation.
No, it's just shameful.
Nobody needs to know."

Peaches and Cream

Over half a century ago
my older brother received his letter
from the local draft board.
He was going to college in a few weeks,
but he still had to get his physical.

That evening he told us the story, chuckling:
the hillbilly guy in front of him,
the doctor's disgust
when he bent over for the rectal exam.

"Well wha'd you expect?"
the hillbilly shot back, annoyed,
"Peaches and cream?"

The phrase entered the family lexicon.
Any time one of us seized up
with revulsion, a cat rounding its back
at an odor, a behavior, a comment,
the response was always,
"What did you expect? Peaches and cream?"

My brother dead more than a decade now,
the war for which we registered
long forgotten, replaced
by others no less pointless,

I remember his death, not even sixty,
a sudden mysterious illness,
his widow falling apart with sorrow,
now in an assisted living facility,
a broken woman, full of guilt and grief.

A second marriage for both,
for a while they'd been so happy,
as if, all along,
they'd expected nothing
but peaches and cream.

After My Brother's Funeral

When I looked
at my reflection
in a storefront
plate-glass window,
I looked older
than I imagined myself,
and shabbier.

New Year's Eve, 2005

Having come back from my first visit
to New Mexico at the start of the month,
to bury my brother,
dead at 57 from a mysterious illness,
I've now gone through North and South
Carolina for the first time,
my wife and I driving
my mother-in-law's Toyota, recently repaired,
back up to Philly,
where she's been a refugee
at her daughter's house
since the hurricane
wiped out her retirement condo,
wrecked her car,
nearly three months before.

We're hoping to make it through
the Capital Beltway traffic
before night falls
and the drunken partiers
come out like vampires
to swoop around 495.

The year is fading
like the late-afternoon light
in the rearview mirror,
missed about as much
as the exit to Bethesda behind us.

A Bumper Year for Ugler Lee

One after another,
family members fell that year,
my uncle in Illinois in February,
in his sleep,
last of his generation;
my father-in-law in Florida, in April,
also in his eighties,
after years of pain;
in May, the first of my generation—
twelve of us grandchildren—
my first cousin Christie, a massive heart attack
in Schenectady, at 61,
same age as her mother
when Aunt Edith collapsed
at the gym after a swim
from her heart attack in 1974,
first of my father's siblings to die.
In December my brother died in Albuquerque,
a mysterious infection
shutting down his organs,
at only fifty-seven.
A bumper year for Ugler Lee, 2005,
picking his victims across the country.
Look at the fat smug bastard,
grinning with self-satisfaction.

O Muse

"At least you should get
a couple of good poems out of this,"
Mary Alice consoled
when I told her about
my cousin's suicide.

She didn't mean it
in a grave-robbing sort of way;
more like a tribute
to the enormity of the event,
as if the poet's burden
to mine experience for nuggets
of poignant detail
were a sort of monument-building.

But still, it struck me
as the last thing that mattered.
When I thought of Teddy
shooting himself in the town cemetery
a thousand miles west of me,
my mother calling with the news,
eight hundred miles to the north,
my brother on the opposite coast
acknowledging the tragedy,
cousins overseas writing to share
their shock, astonishment, distress—
the world shrank to the size of a pea,
and all we did in it –
the working, the fighting,
the fucking, the crying—
so microscopic as to be invisible.

Suicide Poem

"I'm so sorry to hear
about your cousin's suicide,"
Mary Alice cooed,
as if soothing an upset child,
"but at least you should get
a couple of terrific poems out of it."

She made it sound
as if we were bored cats,
waiting for a mouse to scurry past,
wake us to a challenge,
some breathing bauble to bat around
until we lost interest.

What did Mary Alice imagine
I would write about?
The fleeting thoughts in Teddy's head
when he stuck the gun barrel
into his mouth, or
pressed it against his temple,
or to the frog's belly under his chin?
Some remorse about failed relationships?
A dark financial scandal
about to be exposed?

Reflections on life's brevity,
on some unbearable suffering;
and yet how death is never final,
that hole in reality just as potent
as the man whose place it's taken?

Casting the First Stone

"That's just ghoulish,"
Alyson's pronouncement as final as a *fatwa*.
"And he asked your *permission*
to write about your cousin's suicide?"

"It was Albert's decision to write a poem
or not," I conceded, "but he didn't
want to trespass on our friendship,
wipe dogshit on the living room carpet."

"But it's not like he even *knew* your cousin."
When she got on a judgmental roll
there was no stopping her,
as if she were virtue itself,
and I couldn't help remembering
how she'd emptied the joint account
just before she divorced Mark,
the checks he'd bounced
paying the mortgage and phone bill,
her self-righteous justifications afterward
in the face of the hardship she'd put him through.

Nor could I forget
the poem I had written
about Mark kicking her in the gut,
slugging her in the face,
the neighbors pulling him away from her,
Mark spending the night in jail:
the final abuse that caused the divorce.

"Exactly," I said. "It's not as if
he were sullying my cousin's reputation."

Shallow Roots

In the fall the Bradford pear
spills its fruit on the yard,
noisy as a child
seeking its parents' attention.
The hard-barked fruit clack on their way down,
ripping through the still-green leaves,
plop on the ground with the sound
of tossed pebbles,
cover the front walk
like peanut shells
on a happy-hour barroom floor.

Planted twenty years ago,
already taller than the rooftop,
how much longer
can this shallow-rooted tree stand?

Uncle Mike teeters up the steps
to the front porch,
the crunch of the Bradford pears
beneath his shoes
announcing his arrival.
The furrows in his sweaty forehead,
in his blood-red cheeks,
tell his age like tree-rings.

In his mid-sixties,
Mike is his brother Frank's age—
when Frank died,
a weak heart:
like their father before them.

Mishebarach

Midway through the Torah service
the cantor offers a prayer
for those who are ill or suffering.
"May He Who has blessed our forefathers,
Avraham, Yitzchak, and Ya'akov,
bless and heal those who are ill…"
He sweeps his arms around the room
like a lighthouse searchlight swinging out
to illuminate the afflicted.
Congregants call out names.

"Harry Bergman," Rachel Goldstein murmurs
as the cantor's arm sweeps by.
"Alex Kaufman, Avi Katz, Shira Garber,"
Gilbert Stein proclaims, a rescuer
shouting after shipwrecked survivors.
"Shoshona Weiss, Sarah Mankowitz,"
Stephanie Hirsch's phlegm-choked voice croaks,
plaintive as a seagull on the beach.

I wonder at this prayer.
Do we expect miracles from the sky?
Or is it just a simple expression of concern,
a public proclamation of grief?

My cousin lies in a hospital bed in Albany,
a heart attack so massive
it's wiped out her brain function.
The cantor's hand nails me in space.
"Christie Sorum," I whisper,
feeling fraudulent, ineffectual.

His arm completes the arc;
the cantor finishes the prayer:
"May He speedily send
complete recovery from Heaven.
May their recovery be immediate and complete.
And let us say…"

"Amen," the congregation cries out,
complicit in the prayer.

Threshold

The young men in my neighbor's yard,
there to repair a fallen awning,
waved frantically at me
as I pulled out of my driveway,
pointing and calling.
I rolled down the window to hear.
"You have a flat!"

I'd been in denial about this
for several days now,
suspecting the same
but driving on it nevertheless:
it was not pancake flat,
not silly putty pressed against pavement;
I could still drive it to work.

But now I'd been shamed;
I had to get it repaired;
I had no choice.

I thought of the television commercial
for "overactive bladder" medication.
The lady in the ad, "Diane,"
finally decides to consult her doctor
when she finds her need to urinate
interferes with the 60%-off sales
at a local department store.
Enough is enough.

And I remembered my uncle
who delayed attending
to the aneurysm on his aorta
because he didn't want to wake his wife
and waited until morning
to call his doctor,
when it was too late.

Home Again

We didn't exactly rape her,
but Harlow did bring her to the party
with the idea that we'd all fuck her,
Samantha, one of those girls who "pulled trains."
Why not? I was a college freshman
home like a returning warrior
from my first semester on my own
at the college hundreds of miles away,
reuniting with the locals who'd stayed behind.

"Why do I always end up in the bedroom?"
Sam asked plaintively as I pulled on my pants
and Danny entered the bedroom.
I felt like a sneak thief zipping my jeans,
grabbing my boots and easing out the door.
I never saw her again.

Now, forty years later,
I come home from across the country
to find Samantha pushing my mother
in a wheelchair,
helping her bathe and dress,
cooing soothing words to the frail old lady,
a daycare provider for the elderly.
We do not acknowledge our acquaintance—
does she even recognize me?—
but my self-consciousness hangs
between us like a curtain,
suffocating as cotton.

The Tea Party

"Nick was an idiot
when I had him in ninth grade English,
and he's still an idiot," my mother declared
to the guests at the tea party,
in her living room to discuss strategies
for replacing the current mayor,
an anti-government type
who'd spent thirty years
driving a truck for the Parks Department
and figured he knew
all there was to know
about running city government,
with predictable results of mismanagement,
ineptitude, confusion.

"What about Paul Fletcher,
over at the college?" Mom demanded,
her gaze stabbing one guest after the other.
"He's an intelligent person, teaches Poli-Sci.
Can we persuade him to run?
Nick Pasano is *such* an embarrassment."

The tea party guests murmured
general agreement with her,
nodding at one another, taking heart
from the elderly lady speaking her mind.
My mother might not be able
to get to the bathroom by herself, any longer,
but she could still flunk Nick Pasano again
almost half a century later.

Lullabies

When Grandpa's sister died,
Grandma warned us
not to let him know.
He languished in a nursing home,
crippled but still lucid.

"But you're treating him like a baby!"
I cried to my mother,
"She's his sister! He *has* to know!"

"It's Grandma's decision," Mama scolded me,
neither agreeing nor disputing;
I thought of soldiers explaining
they were only following orders.

"Grandma doesn't want to remind him
the last time he saw Eleanor
he ordered her from the house.
Of course, he didn't mean what he said."
Mama's eyes shifted away from mine.

Sunday after Sunday we visited Grandpa,
telling our cheery school tales,
the books we'd been reading,
the games we'd been playing.
I felt the duplicity snake
like poison through my body.
Grandpa shrank and shrank in my sight
until I knew he was just a baby in a crib.

Tribute to Steve

We grieved when our cat died,
93 or 94 in feline years, according
to a chart on the vet's wall.

In some respects, a burden lifted:
no longer having to witness his decline,
no more twice-daily pills poked
down forced-open jaws.
Signs of his incontinence remain on the rug.

But within weeks mice infested our home,
at first just a whisper of feet in the walls,
a spray of droppings in dark basement corners.
Emboldened by Steve's absence,
they moved on to the kitchen,
like a group of New Year's Eve revelers.

In no time they were brazen as whores
lifting their skirts at midnight to passing cars:
they nibbled crackers and chewed through boxes,
tore open cellophane-wrapped packages of cookies.
My daughter returned late from babysitting
one Saturday night to find
a mouse dancing across the kitchen counter.
In the morning I discovered
a loaf of bread shredded to confetti.

I set traps in the pantry, smeared
with chocolate, cheese and peanut butter.
In the morning my wife found the corpse,
spread out on the lazy Susan,
its neck snapped in the sprung trap.
Abby woke me to dispose of the body,
in her mind a man's job.

The stiff rodent seemed a child's toy;
my children refused to look at the broken doll,
horrified we'd killed it, the brutish reality
Steve shielded us from all those years.

The Bequest

Out on the porch, Oscar poked his cane,
like an andiron stirring dead coals,
into the cardboard boxes
destined for the yard sale,
the junk heap.

"Fifty years of things.
All that memory.
And now all I can do
is throw it out."
His voice nearly broke.

An eighty-seven-year-old widower,
three months removed
from heart surgery,
his ribcage pulled apart
like a cracked lobster shell,
Oscar could no longer live alone.
His daughter grudged him a room,
as if he were already dust.

From a box, Oscar rescued a brass menorah
as if recovering a body from a crypt,
passed it to my wife and me.
"Here. You take this."

Then the movers pulled up to the curb.
"Ready to roll, Pops?"

Part Four: Palliative Care

Palliative Care

It wasn't a term he'd ever heard
when the hospital official on the telephone—
did she say her name was Watson? Watkins?—
called to discuss his mother's condition.

This was the nightmare he'd had for years,
after his father died over a decade before,
the shrill telephone in the middle of the night
summoning him to the news of disaster,
the stark bedpan voice on the line,
all metal and glass.

Only, the call came on a sunny afternoon by the lake
and – did she say her name was Watkins?—
didn't mention Armageddon, only
the "option" of palliative care,

and when he looked the term up online—
from the Latin *palliare,* "to cloak"—
it didn't say anything about euthanasia,
just a focus on relieving suffering,
including *treatment for curable illnesses,*
only a cursory mention of the word "hospice."

Institutional Hell

After checking in with my mother
in her room at the hospital,
we went to the "conference room"—
so like a snack area with pastel walls,
molded plastic chairs and vending machines,
another version of institutional hell—
where a hirsute nurse in loose blue scrubs named Roland,
chest hair like tumbleweeds erupting from his collar,
arms sprouting fur like a chia pet—
a hairy spider, the very embodiment of Ugler Lee—
discussed palliative care options with us.
He made me think of a hitman for the mob.

The bottom line was she wanted to die
at home, looking out of the sliding glass door
at the Kalamazoo River flowing by,
the familiar home sounds of the refrigerator's hum,
the overhead fans in the background.

Since falling in the bathroom,
an agony of three months in the nursing home,
its soul-killing antiseptic atmosphere
among drooling end-of-lifers,
she'd begged to stay home,
schemed to that end, spending a fortune
renovating the bathroom:
elevated toilet, handrails, the shower—
which she did not enter unaccompanied—
a step-in affair with a sturdy chair to sit on.

At least we were able to get her back
to her home for the last two days of her life,
not that she was aware of her surroundings,
only buoyed by a desire to die.

86

Bacon

After we discussed my mother's treatment wishes
with Roland, the nurse from the palliative care unit,
as if we were talking mutual funds and IRA's
with our financial planner, confusing details
about the requirements of home hospice care,
"heroic" measures, the alleviation of pain,
decisions as tricky as walking through a minefield,
searching Roland's face for clues
to the "right answers,"

we went back to my mom's room,
where she lay all dopey-eyed and drooling
against a propped-up pillow on the adjustable bed.
One more night in the hospital
before she'd be driven back home in an ambulance
to spend her final days.

"And what would she like for her last breakfast
with us tomorrow before she goes?"
The nurse, pencil in hand, poised over her pad,
looked at us as if asking after a Death Row inmate's
final meal before execution.

"I think she'd like a strip of bacon," I began,
remembering my mother's fondness for it,
but immediately the nurse was shaking her head.

"No, she can't have bacon.
Cured meats are bad for the lung function
and increase the risk of lung disease."

My mom would be dead within days
and they were worried about lung disease?

Britches

In her nineties,
when she could no longer
get to the bathroom on her own,
her knees no longer reliable,
after the botched knee replacement,
like the tops of jars that don't really fit,
she'd call neighbors to help her
out of her recliner, into her wheelchair,
a system of positioned walkers and railings
to help her keep her balance,
get her from here to there.

To begin the process,
she pressed the button
that lowered the recliner forward
while her assistants restrained her,
kept her from sliding to the floor.

"Hitch my britches!" she'd command,
implore, in a sort of joking tone,
using the quaint, archaic word
to deflect the shame she felt,
the humiliation she endured,
as her helper put his hand
down into the back of her waistband,
grabbed a fistful of intimate apparel,
hoisted her to standing,
until she could hold onto the walker,
a stranded swimmer clinging to a raft.

The Chair

After she could no longer sleep in her bed
for fear of not being able to get up from it—
she had to call friends to get her to her feet
several mornings one week, the panic and shame
scalding her like hot water—
Mom bought an electric-powered recliner
like some space-age furniture from *Star Trek,*
a push-button control panel to lift, lower, eject,
little blinking red and green power lights,
maybe even a bell or a beep,
firm leather cushions befitting a pasha.

She spent most of her time in its lap,
either asleep, reading, or watching television,
with excursions to the bathroom,
the table in the breakfast nook by the kitchen window.

Once when there was a power failure overnight,
she'd been trapped like an insect in a Venus flytrap,
neighbors having to come take the chair apart,
get her into a wheelchair and roll her to the bathroom,
putting it back together when power was restored.

When she died,
neither my brother nor I
could bring ourselves to sit there.
The empty chair beckoned,
but it just didn't feel right
to sink into those cushions.

End Game

Helping my mother to the bathroom—
recently renovated with handrails,
an elevated toilet seat,
after her fall and nursing home stay
a few months earlier—
reinforces my sadness
at her inevitable, irreversible decline,
and I remember as vivid as yesterday
forty-five years back
when she had to scrape gobs of shit
from her senile, bed-ridden father,
my job at the time to roll him over
while she went to work with washcloth and soap.

To me, my grandfather seemed
a fossil from legend,
a barnacle of age
clinging to youth,
leeching its vitality.

Mom wasn't yet fifty then,
but the look on her face,
which I mistook for anger—
eyebrows knitting together in concentration,
eyes like hard marbles,
mouth pursed to a line-laced frown—
was the awareness of what one day
would be her fate, too.
And mine.

The House She Died In

When we moved into the house
by the river, in 1954,
the same neighbors who'd be there
when my mother died fifty-eight years later
already lived on either side,
Steve and Marion on one side,
Herm and Betty on the other—
though Betty and Steve had both died
in the intervening decades,
as had my father;
Herm had lost his marbles to Alzheimer's
and Marion frail as an ancient housecat.

Now the house to which I returned
for over four decades since I left home,
is like a black hole
in the universe of my childhood,
the river behind it flowing
endlessly into the future.

An Appliance

"I want to die!" my mother croaked,
the voice toneless but determined.
The EMTs had just wheeled her into the house,
strapped like a corpse to the gurney,
as if they were delivering an appliance
from a department store truck.

We got her situated in the hospital bed
we'd set up in the dining room the day before,
mattress cranked to a reclining position,
guard rails up so she wouldn't fall out.

This was where she would die,
at home, as she'd wanted,
but to hear her lament, her one single wish,
felt like a rock crushing my chest.

We've all said it, haven't we?
Histrionic hyperbole when circumstances
seem to be conspiring against us,
as if we were merely the butt
of some cosmic practical joke,
knowing all along we don't mean it,
not really.

But my mother did mean it.
Really.
There was just this one way
out of her suffering, now.

Headstone

"Everybody knows I was born July 30, 1919,"
my mother observed, amused,
"if they bothered to look at the marker."

When my father died,
back in the last century,
they had one headstone made
since their ashes would be interred
side by side, facing the Kalamazoo River
in their plot in Riverside Cemetery,
elevated on a little hill
like a couple in the front row
of a drive-in movie.

She wasn't one to lie about her age,
but still, she thought it funny
in a macabre, gallows-humor sort of way,
as if she were advertising on a billboard.

Eighteen years later my family—
wife, daughters, cousins—
celebrated with her on a sunny July 30,
her 93rd this time—
less than two weeks before she died,
August 11, 2012, the date
to be carved into the marble,
like a period at the end of a sentence.

Sammy

My brother and I joked
our ninety-year-old mother eloped
with her caregiver, Sam.
He'd been looking after her
the last ten years,
at once her savior—
dear as family—
and the bane of her existence—
again, just like family.

Two years behind us in school,
we'd known Sam all our lives,
though we hadn't been friends
when we lived in the same town.

Related to half of the town, it seemed,
Sam had never married,
devoted himself to his brothers and sisters,
now the exclusive companion of our mom,
driving her to endless doctors' appointments,
 buying her groceries, preparing her meals,
writing her checks, managing her life:
as time went on and she became more helpless,
weak as a kitten if tiger-fierce,
Sam did more: cut her meat,
 got her to the bathroom,
helped her dress:
everything but bathe her.

My brother and I, on opposite coasts,
thousands of miles away from her,
in the northern Midwest,
visited several times a year,
called weekly, wrote letters, but
Sam was with her every day.

And when she was dying,
it was Sam she sought for comfort,
as if a spiritual husband,
to relieve her pains, soothe her fears,
ease her into death,
Sam to whom she pleaded
for her life to end.

Averting a Calamity

In the Subject line of the email, I wrote:
"I've fallen down and I can't get up,"
having just seen a commercial
for one of those emergency notification services
for elderly people living alone,
an alert button like a dog collar around the neck:
flimsy acting, a woman reclining
like an odalisque in a tub,
as if enjoying a bubble bath,
a man lying on the ground in a park,
very preppy in a cardigan and chinos,
head propped in his palm,
elbow on the grass,
both speaking to the camera
as if reading from a teleprompter,
neither looking particularly in pain.

I meant to send the email to myself,
a reminder to write a poem
about my mom at the age of 92,
falling off the toilet, breaking her hip.
She'd lived alone for fifteen years
since my father died,
a thousand miles away from where I lived.

She called her caregiver, Sammy,
who later described her agony to me,
when he drove her to the emergency room.

When I tried to insert my email address
from the address book,
I clicked the rabbi's email instead,
"Ravdaniel" right below mine.

I noticed my error five minutes later,
quickly sent an explanation, beginning "Oops…."

The rabbi wrote back,
"Ha! Glad to hear you're OK."

The Noose

A voracious reader
with an omnivorous appetite—
literature, murder mysteries, biographies,
book reviews, news magazines—
my mother felt the noose tighten
when her eyes began to fail,
the vision blurry, her head throbbing.

The knees, the kidneys, the arthritis—
these she had come to terms with,
like the amicable reconciliation
of a separating couple—
but her eyesight!

Housebound, chairbound, unable to move,
only books to free her
from the chains of her diminishment,
what could take the place of her eyes?

Glaucoma blurred her vision
like a sledgehammer to the head.
"Doctor Lal says the pressure
has gone down since he last measured,"
she reported over the phone,
as if there were some hope
she might overcome this newest obstacle.

After My Mother Died

After my mother died and we sold her house,
Marcus West reminisced that fifty years back
he'd received his first blow job
in my bed,
one summer afternoon
when my parents were away
and my older brother David,
himself dead these past seven years,
had organized a private poker party
with some of our high school buddies,
complete with a couple cases of beer.
I must have been away, too;
Dave threw poker parties
whenever my parents left town,
an excuse to drink beer.

I didn't know whether to be sick
or congratulatory—*Way to go, Marcus!*—
wondering vaguely if I'd slept
in the same bed
before the sheets had been changed,
a vision of germs and jism
flashing through my middle-aged brain.

When Marcus told me who did it,
I just felt sick.
Nancy Flanders was my girlfriend.

Two Mothers

Two months after my mother died,
my mother-in-law had a stroke
in her assisted living facility in Florida,
like a circuit-breaker switch snapping.
She fell, hit her head,
blood staining her brain.
Somebody found her a few hours later,
called 911—and her daughters.

Like a road sign, this marked
the beginning of the end,
just as surely as my mother's meltdown in August,
both women frail nonagenarians.

A sneaky feeling of relief settled on me,
like some comic book superhero's
shroud of invincibility, his protective amulet:
I'd already been through this,
couldn't lose my mom again;
no more fear of the dreaded phone call,
ice-water shocking at three in the morning,
delivering the prosaic fact
that somehow changes everything.

The Gematria of Five Sisters

The rabbi hadn't known my mother-in-law.
Associated with Beth Israel Memorial Chapel,
he buried Jews all the time, his job.

So when he began the service
noting Ruth had been born February twenty-second, 1920,
her daughters immediately corrected him:
February second, Groundhogs Day, James Joyce's birthday.

"But the email said the twenty-second,"
he protested, the big gray beard
a kabuki mask hiding his intention.
Did he hope to persuade them
their mother really had been born on that date?
Shifting the blame, claiming innocence?

All at once, I figured he must have written
a neat little sermon
based on a gematria riff on the number 22—
"all things" in Hebrew numerology,
the number of letters in the alphabet—
unless his verbal jujitsu had to do
with the Jewish calendar;
he *did* allude to the month of Adar, after all—
which was also wrong.

Ruth's daughters insisted on the facts,
and to his credit, the rabbi elided seamlessly
to a reflection on the gift of children,
living survivors who preserve
the memories of their parents.
Five daughters, count 'em.

The Minyan

"Goldie's here," my sister-in-law announced,
peering out of the family room into the chapel
where the funeral guests shuffled in, took seats,
mostly older ladies pushing walkers.

"That's so kind of her," another sister admired.
"She and Mom had had a falling out
over some detail of Jewish law."
An understatement: Goldie and Ruth
hadn't spoken to each other in more than a year,
having argued over some obscure point
of kashrut during Pesach, two springs back,
shrill voices shouting over each other
across their mutual deafness
and blind self-certainty.

But yes, I thought, it *was* nice that death
could resolve petty differences
in a show of unconditional love,
show the way to what was really important.

The guests having arrived,
the funeral director guided us into the chapel,
showed us to our seats.

"There's not even a *minyan*,"
I heard Goldie's dismissive murmur
in the silence of the sanctuary,
and, noting I was only one of three males
among the two dozen mourners,
I reflected the word means "count" in Hebrew,
refers to the quorum of Jewish adults
required for certain religious rites.

So this was why they'd had the "falling out."
Goldie was a bully;
but so was my mother-in-law.
Neither could tolerate
being bossed by somebody else,
each a minyan of one.

The Tribute

Four months after my mother died,
a handful of Christmas cards drifted in
like leaves from far-flung trees.

I wrote a note to each,
delivering the news.

Six weeks later an envelope
from an unfamiliar name in New Hampshire
came through the mail slot in the front door
like a knife blade into flesh.

"I have a secret to share with you,"
the note began.
"When a credit card company prompts me
for the name of my favorite teacher,
I answer 'Rammelkamp.'"

Twenty years after my father died,
thirty since he retired,
this former student,
a grown man with a wife and children,
a life of his own,
continued to stay in touch with my mother,
and I know nobody
will ever remember me
with such fondness,
a realization at once humbling and proud.

The Return of Ugler Lee

Years later, after my father
had been almost two decades dead,
my brother and I remembered
some of his foibles, his idiosyncrasies,
passions, obsessions—
books, cats, JFK, the *Saint Louis Post-Dispatch*—
his tender stomach, his tender heart—
and we returned to the concept of Ugler Lee.

Ugler Lee the grim reaper,
Ugler Lee the lethal bogeyman,
the terror of our dreams,
the cause of cold sweat,
Ugler Lee who comes a-callin'
like a thief in the middle of the night,
a thief in broad daylight,
and there's no way to resist.
Be not proud, Ugler Lee.

That summer Ugler Lee got cozy
with our mother.
Ugler Lee will be coming for us next.

He Adored Her

"I rode the train with your father
from Springfield to Chicago in 1940
when he went back to graduate school at Brown,"
my Aunt Jane reminisced
in her condolence card,
after my mother died.

"All the way to Union Station he demanded,
'Isn't she the most beautiful girl?
Isn't she the most perfect girl that ever was?
How can I go away and leave her?'
He was just desperately in love
and never ceased to be."

I could picture Aunt Jane,
my father's first cousin,
with whom he'd grown up,
frail now herself,
virtually the last of her generation,
remembering that train ride to Chicago,
vivid as yesterday,
the clack of the wheels against the rails,
my father's desperation,
the life force propelling them
ever forward, into the future.

Meeting My Mother in the Hereafter

"Why'd you leave me like that,
after the EMTs wheeled me into the house?
You could have stayed a couple days longer;
it wouldn't have killed you.
I felt like you were abandoning me!
There I was, dying, and nobody to look out for me
except Sammy."

"I hadn't come out to Michigan for a funeral,"
I protested lamely, basically feeling lucky,
even in the face of my mother's guilt-tripping.
Here I was, *in Heaven.* Who'd have guessed?
I mean, I'm a sucker for a happy ending,
but never in my wildest dreams did I imagine
life-after-death was going to be like this!
"All I had packed was jeans and t-shirts.
I was on vacation!
We had to get Zoe back for the MCAT.
Besides, Bob was flying in from LA later that day."

"I wanted both my boys with me.
We'd planned that for October, remember?
Just the three of us. You could have stayed.
Abby could have driven Zoe back to Baltimore."

"I came back for your funeral," I mumbled,
eyes lowered. On some level, she was right,
but here we were,
and I couldn't help smiling.

"But I was already dead then,
and for all you knew, you'd never see me again.
You were always the big atheist,
didn't believe in God or Heaven,
Mr. Existentialist. Mr. Nihilist."

I hung my head.

"Come here, give me a kiss."

Part Five: End of the Line

The Ambassadors

"That's where the hotel was,
where Bobby Kennedy was shot,"
my twin brother points
to a huge public school administration building
as we walk along Wilshire Blvd.
There's a plaque on the sidewalk honoring RFK.

"Remember that? We were in high school,
woke up on our birthday to learn
he'd been shot the night before
after winning the California primary."

"Yeah, a couple of months after Doctor King,"
I nodded, remembering our Michigan childhood.
"Then in November Nixon beat Ho-hum Humphrey
and that bigot George Wallace,
who'd also been shot that year.
Crazy times."

"The city asked the family
if it was OK to tear down the hotel," Bob says.
"The Coconut Grove used to be in the Ambassador, too.
All kinds of celebrities – Errol Flynn, Clark Gable,
Cary Grant, Marlene Dietrich."
He waves his hand in a big arc
to indicate the galaxy of stars.

My daughter and I are in LA
this Veterans' Day weekend
to visit my brother
who is about to start chemotherapy:
Stage Four lung cancer.
Crazy times indeed.

Gemini

You expect it and expect it and expect it,
but when death comes,
you didn't expect it at all.

Bob had been fighting cancer for years,
a losing battle against a stronger opponent,
mano-a-mano through five rounds of chemo,
radiation, opdivo, pain management,
addiction to opiates,

and all along the Cain and Abel struggle,
the Jacob and Esau conflict,
after which, one of us would still be standing,
for a little while, at least.

Seven weeks shy of sixty-four,
the Beatles' milestone for old age,
me with a grandchild on my knee,
he with a widow and pet iguana.

And a lifetime of memories,
not all good,
that I shall scrimp and save.

Six Months

When I spoke to my sister-in-law that Friday
she said the doctors had told her
six months: how much longer
her husband had to live. My twin brother.

Bob was being sent home from St. Vincent's
in Los Angeles, for hospice care.
I spoke to him briefly; he sounded exhausted.
I promised to call after he got home.

Spring Sunday in Baltimore,
the dogwoods and cherry blossoms
just coming into bloom.
Sitting on the front porch, I resolved
to call Bob later that afternoon.
I had six months, right?

But then my daughter stopped by
with her husband and baby,
out for a stroll on a lovely afternoon:
my first grandchild,
not yet three months old.

By the time they left,
it was getting to be dinner time.
I needed to tend to the lentil soup
I was preparing; I would call Bob tomorrow,
I told myself. *Six months.*

When I called Los Angeles the next day,
Lourdes told me he'd died early that morning.

Zen Riddle

After my credit card was canceled
for attempted identity theft—
"Your card's been compromised,"
the euphemistic explanation—
a replacement number issued,
I had to call various places—
EZ Pass, public radio, the power company, etc.—
to update my information
for the periodic account charges,
which was when I encountered security questions
whose answers I didn't necessarily remember.

The name of the elementary school I attended,
the name of my first pet,
my favorite rock and roll band.
The name of my favorite nephew?
How many had I had when I was asked?
What name did I say? Eli? Henry?

"What is the name of the nearest city
in which a sibling of yours lives?"

When did I answer that one?
"Both of my brothers are dead,"
I told the operator,
while "Nirvana," "Heaven," "Hell"
all shuffled through my head.

"But maybe the answer's Los Angeles."
David died in Albuquerque,
eleven years ahead of Bob,
closer to Baltimore than LA,
but could this security question
really be that old?

What is the sound of one hand clapping?
Say it to exorcize it.
Say "I love you" so you can feel the doubt.

About the Author

Charles Rammelkamp is Prose Editor for BrickHouse Books in Baltimore, where he lives with his wife, Abby. The two are retired from federal government service. Rammelkamp is the author of several collections of "historical" or "biographical" poetry sequences, written in dramatic monologue form, including *Fusen Bakudan* (Time Being Books), about World War Two Japanese balloon bombs and leper colony missionaries in Vietnam; *Mata Hari: Eye of the Day* (Apprentice House), about the life and career of the World War I *femme fatale* spy; *American Zeitgeist* (Apprentice House), which deals with the populist politician and Scopes Trial buffoon, William Jennings Bryan; *Catastroika* (Apprentice House), another collection of dramatic monologues in the voices of Maria Rasputin, the mad monk's daughter, who escaped Russia after the Revolution and became a lion tamer for Ringling Brothers, and a fictional Jewish character, Sasha Federmesser, who likewise escapes and immigrates to Baltimore. A chapbook of poems about female sailors in the British Royal Navy during the 17th and 18th centuries, *Jack Tar's Lady Parts* (Main Street Rag Press), is also written in this style.

www.ingramcontent.com/pod-product-compliance
Lightning Source LLC
Chambersburg PA
CBHW022011080426
42733CB00007B/567